Index

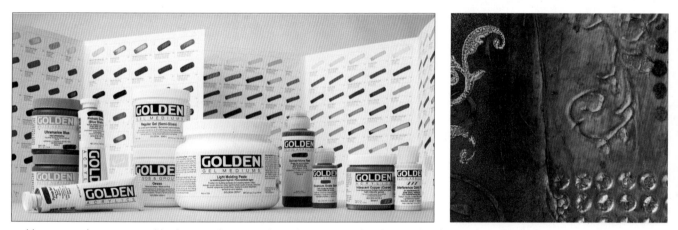

Golden Artist Colors gives a visible clue as to the paint color in the containers by placing a hand-painted swatch of color on each and every label of its paints. You can actually see the transparency or opaqueness, sheen, and color quality of the paint. Keep your eyes open!

Acrylic Basics

Acrylic paints and products are water soluble ... that means easy to clean up. Remove excess paint or product from your brush with a rag or paper towel and then rinse your brush thoroughly between applications. This will keep the acrylic from drying permanently on your brush. At the end of your session, wash your brushes with warm water and a little soap.

If you want to "thin" your acrylic paint, use a polymer medium instead of water. Adding water to thin the paints gives an interesting effect, but causes the paint film to be uneven. Just decide ahead of time what look you are going after!

By using different amounts of water on your brush you will create varied results. A damp brush is best when desiring full coverage and an even coat. For watercolor effects, use a wet brush. A dry brush will result in a more "hit and miss" paint film, which is also effective.

Always read labels. A few pigments and products contain elements that may be hazardous to you or to the environment. Be proactive in keeping yourself safe.

Thin coats of acrylic paint or product will dry very quickly, making it easy to build up multiple color layers. Thick coats need time to dry completely. They will form a "skin" on the surface but may still be wet underneath. Be patient!

When first using artist grade paints, go sparingly to learn the true strength of the pigments. You will be surprised how far a little paint will go and how strong the color truly is. You will find this a valuable tip when mixing tints, pastels and blends.

Water Soluble... Easy Clean Up!

Handy Tools: *Applying Paints, Mediums, Gels, Grounds & Pastes*

Small textures added with beads

Fine swirls created with a toothpick

Cookie cutter circle imprints

Brush strokes made with flat edged brush

Raised web pattern created by pulling up on wet paint with a diamond palette knife

Palette knife paint application

Circles made with jar lids

Lines created with fork

Pointed stick marks

Larger "dots" created using end of pencil or eraser

Hatch marks and concentric circle swirls are made with a rubber Graining tool

More "toothpick" marks

Pattern created with a foam stamp

Marks made with a "color shaper"

This painting has two underlying products upon which the marks were made: the left side is Molding Paste; the right side is Heavy Body Titan Buff.

The marks were made into or onto the wet products and then allowed to dry. You will notice that the marks made into the Molding Paste are deeper and more sculpted, while those made into the paint are more subtle.

The piece was then painted using Fluid Acrylics in transparent pigments ... Indian Yellow Hue, Nickel Azo Yellow, Transparent Pyrrole Orange, Green Gold, and Quinacridone Burnt Orange.

No need for a lot of expensive, fancy tools! A few basic brushes, markers and textured items are all you need for fabulous results.

Brushes: It is important to have a number of brushes that are sturdy and are made for use with acrylic paint. I prefer flat or angled brushes because of the way in which I paint. You will find which works best for your style.

Since your brush needs to be washed frequently (because you don't want the paint to dry on your brush), keep in mind the construction of the brush. I need to "reglue" my brushes to their handles periodically as they become loose from use. This is easy to do and saves having to buy new brushes!

Inexpensive "chip" brushes from the local hardware store are great for applying gesso, mediums and gels, and for "scrubbing" the paint into rough textures. These have a tendency to lose bristles so check carefully that you haven't left one behind on your work! Foam brushes are also handy to have around and are easy to find as well as inexpensive. I like to use their round handles to make circle marks into my work for subtle texture.

Other Mark Makers: Tools that are made for removing paint cleanly are called "color shapers." They have various rubber tips that remove the top layer of paint (while wet) to reveal what is underneath. They are fun to use and come in sets.

There is a great little item that is a "graining" tool. Each side has different teeth and it makes great line patterns in paint.

Toothpicks, chopsticks, forks, combs, palette knives, wooden rulers, and pencils with erasers … you already have these; try using them to make marks!

Sponges: I cannot be without the small triangle-shaped makeup sponges (Cut N Dry Foam works great too). I use them for stenciling, to apply paint to foam stamps, to make marks, etc. Sea sponges are also great to use with acrylics as they have an irresistibly irregular texture to their surface!

Palette Knives: A couple of broad angle palette knives are a really good investment because they are practical and valuable for many purposes. Buy the plastic ones as they clean up well and don't rust. They cost very little and are worth their weight in gold. The diamond shaped knife is useful for getting interesting "web" patterns in heavy body paints and products and for applying paint and gels.

Stencils & Stamps: I am always on the lookout for nonrepresentational stencils and stamps. What do I mean by this? I want patterns and textures for these, not boats, birds, or butterflies! I've been fortunate to be a "stencil" person for a long time, so I have a lot of old ones that I use regularly.

Go through your collections and glean out the ones that provide pattern and can work to give you texture. I look for geometrics, classic architectural designs, swirls, tiles, etc. Foam stamps are an absolute gift to those of us who like to manipulate products to create dips and crevices. These inexpensive tools are easily found and come in a variety of shapes.

Circle Cutters: I stumbled upon a set of graduated biscuit/cookie cutters in a restaurant supply store a few years ago and they are fabulous. I apply paint to the thick, rolled edge of the cutter and stamp it onto my work. I can easily get the same size circle every time! How great is that?

Applying Paints and Products does not require a lot of expensive, fancy tools!

Acrylic Pigment Reality

Understanding pigments will allow you to make the most of your efforts...

This "lesson" is crucial to helping you make the most out of your painting experience and will guide you in making paint selections that are ideal for achieving your desired results.

Like everyone else learning something new, I made lots of "mud" in my early color mixing days, so I would like to share what I learned so you can get out of the mud, too.

Pigments provide the color for all artist paint: acrylic, oil and watercolors. In acrylic paint these pigments are suspended in a finely-tuned polymer medium that is

White when it is Wet, but
Clear when it is Dry.

The polymer medium forms a film after the water evaporates. This film, sometimes referred to as a skin, is what we see when acrylic paint dries on a surface to which it has been applied. These skins get their color from the various pigments that are mixed with the polymer mediums.

Enhance opaque paints by applying transparent glazes on top to create mood, texture and shadows.

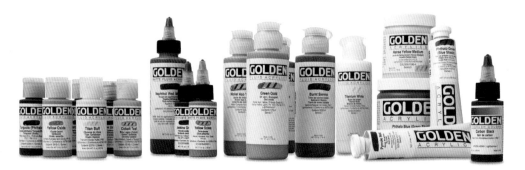

Pigments come from two sources:

Mineral Pigments are harvested from natural sources here on earth such as soils, minerals, metals, and ores. They have names such as Siennas, Umbers, Cobalts, Cadmiums, Chromiums and others.

Try to picture these pigments as finely ground up dirt, rocks, metals or minerals. Since these are not transparent in their natural state, light cannot pass through them; therefore, the paints produced from them will be opaque.

When the paint film is dried you can expect to see good coverage and very little, if any, surface sheen. I think of these colors as "grounding" colors as they provide a wonderful basis upon which to build other color layers.

Choose these colors when you want to
Color and Cover at the same time.

Modern Pigments are created in a chemistry lab and generally carry long complicated names like Quinacridones, Phthalos, and Diarylides. They have a very different structure than the mineral pigments. Imagine the modern pigments as slivers of stained glass, transparent and glossy.

The paints made from these pigments are also transparent and glossy. Because the light can actually pass through these sheer pigments, they are perfect for layering, glazing, and creating subtle blends of color without losing your ability to see through to the underlying layers below.

Choose these colors when you want to
Color without Covering.

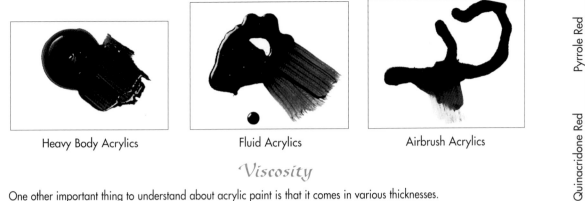

Heavy Body Acrylics   Fluid Acrylics   Airbrush Acrylics

Viscosity

One other important thing to understand about acrylic paint is that it comes in various thicknesses.

We call this **Viscosity**.

The paints called **Heavy Body Acrylics** that are sold in tubes or jars are one of the thickest or most viscous of the acrylic line. They will retain brush strokes, marks, and texture, and give excellent coverage when used full strength. They can be applied with a brush or palette knife and are somewhat akin to toothpaste in consistency.

Fluid Acrylics are much looser and less viscous than the Heavy Body colors, but are equal in pigment. Ounce for ounce, the Fluids have the same amount of pigment as the denser, more viscous Heavy Body line. With the Fluids you get a smoother application, more leveling, less visible textures left from brushes and applicators, and the ability to make a fine line with no drag on your brush and no diluting. In addition, you can drop, drip, and pour this paint!

The least viscous is the **Airbrush** line. The paints are extremely thin, though highly pigmented. Airbrush Acrylics are great for staining, for use as water media, as inks and, of course, with an airbrush for which they were originally formulated.

Fresh brewed tea - transparent

Milk added - cloudy

Tea & Milk Analogy

How to avoid "muddy" mixes or
How to Color but not completely Cover:

I want you to imagine making a cup of fresh hot tea. The rich amber color of the tea is a perfect way to visualize a modern transparent pigment such as Quinacridone/Nickel Azo Gold.

When the tea is just brewed it is the color of sheer transparent amber, and even when we add a touch of honey (another sheer fluid) to the tea, the transparency is still maintained. So far we have not "muddied" up our tea, only slightly altered the amber color. We can still see through it.

Similarly, it follows that by adding another sheer transparent color to our original Quinacridone/Nickel Azo Gold we would NOT produce a muddy mix, but would alter or enhance the original color with the addition of another sheer color which would lend color to our work, but not hide or cover underlying layers.

But, if we decided to add milk (a cloudy, opaque liquid, certainly not transparent) to our cup of clear amber tea, the tea immediately clouds up and gets muddy.

The clear transparent amber color becomes a brownish white through which it becomes difficult to see. Following this analogy, if we take our original Quinacridone/Nickel Azo Gold paint and ADD an opaque, mineral color such as Titan Buff to it, the result will be a cloudy or muddy color which has lost its transparent quality and would now both color and cover our work, obscuring the underlying layers fully or partially.

A Note About Final Coats: I have not addressed the details of final protective coats or varnish coats in this small book. I fully recommend that, if you are producing art for sale, you learn the ins and outs of this important process. Varnish coats protect your work from dust and dirt as well as from exposure to ultraviolet light. Since they are removable, your painting can be cleaned if the surface should become dirty or damaged over time.

Pyrrole Red

Quinacridone Red

Chromium Oxide Green

Green Gold

Yellow Ochre

Nickel Azo Yellow

Cobalt Blue

Phthalo Blue (Red Shade)

Burnt Sienna

Quinacridone/ Nickel Azo Gold

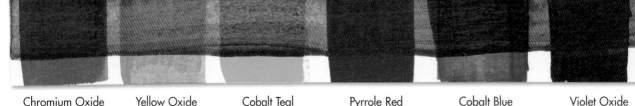

Quinacridone/Nickel Azo Gold is painted over these colors.

Modern over Mineral

| Chromium Oxide Green | Yellow Oxide | Cobalt Teal | Pyrrole Red | Cobalt Blue | Violet Oxide |

Unravel the Mystery of Color Mixing

Layering Colors   *Modern over Mineral lets you see both, but Mineral over Modern hides what's below.*

Cool & Warm Colors

Colors are not only mineral or modern, they are transparent or opaque; and they are also warm and cool in appearance.

This is fairly easy to envision. Imagine a line of colors which reflect your understanding of actual warm and cool temperatures:

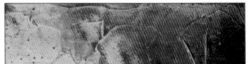

Warm being "seen" on this line as Red

Warm being seen as fire in Red and Yellow and Orange, it is warm to hot in temperature.

Cool being "seen" on this line as Blue

Cool can easily be visualized as ice and water. As we imagine cool things, we see Blues, Aquas and Purples.

But did you also realize that a Red, for example, can either be a Cool Red or a Warm Red? A Quinacridone Red is a Cool Red with the underlying tones tending toward the Blue side, whereas a Naphthol Red is a Warm Red with definite Orange and Yellow undertones.

It is always important to explore your paints with an eye to the overall impression a color can give you. When you select a group of colors for a project, keep this in mind. A single color choice can make all the difference.

Invest the time in the beginning checking out the properties of each color you own. It's worth it.

Using Whites to Make Color Changes

Quinacridone/Nickel Azo
Gold with Indian Yellow Hue

Quinacridone/Nickel Azo
Gold with Indian Yellow
Hue plus Titan Buff

Quinacridone/Nickel Azo
Gold with Indian Yellow Hue
with more Titan Buff

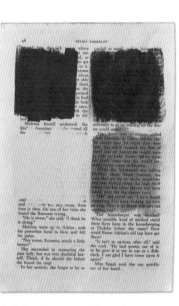

Left Side - Titanium White plus your choice of colors makes a semi-opaque mixture that almost hides the words.

Right Side - Your choice of a Modern/transparent color (with no White added) painted over the words is almost transparent and lets you see the words.

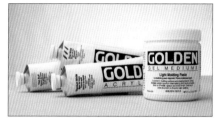

Titanium White   Zinc White   Titan Buff
Light Molding Paste

How to Mix a Tint:
Hansa Yellow Medium plus
Titanium White makes a soft
Pastel Yellow "Tint"

Titanium White

Titan Buff

Light Molding Paste

Zinc White

Titanium White +
Quinacridone Red

Titan Buff +
Quinacridone Red

Light Molding Paste
+ Quinacridone Red

Zinc White +
Quinacridone Red

Why Different Whites?

Most of us understand that when we want to lighten a color we add white. It seems fairly simple and straightforward. The more white you add, the lighter the tint or pastel. With less white, the opposite occurs.

Titanium White is the best choice of white paint to use to create simple straightforward pastels and for color lightening purposes. It is an opaque, stark and clear white, which will lighten any other color, Mineral or Modern, and increase the opacity of Modern colors. You will get clear bright pastels and tints that **Color and Cover.**

Light Molding Paste will achieve the same results as white paint and also add texture. Although not a paint, it is a thick paste that is very white. It will give you a lot of texture as well as achieving lightening of color, good coverage and clear bright pastels that **Color And Cover.**

Zinc White is a third white which is NOT opaque, but translucent. It is known as a "glazing" white and will make sheer pastels and tints with a see-through quality, a bit frosty in appearance to **Color without Covering**.

Titan Buff is the last white on my list, but it is never least in my choices. Titan Buff is not really white. It is a light linen-colored opaque paint which, when mixed with other colors, makes warmer pastels with a "bleached" or sun-washed look. Pastels from Titan Buff and your choice of colors will be soft and aged. They **Color and Cover!**

TIP: The key to mixing your pastels is to add the color slowly, drawing in the white and the color a bit at a time until you arrive at the desired color strength. Remember you can always make a pastel stronger by adding more color to white. That way you won't end up with a cup full of Pale Pink because you poured out too much Red to start with!

Squeeze a drop of color and a drop of white onto a mixing surface.

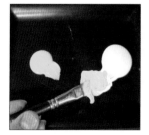

Use a brush or mixing knife to add just a bit of color to the drop of white.

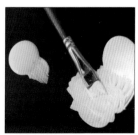

Mix the bit of color into the white. The color will alter the white rapidly.

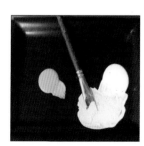

Add a second color to white for a different shade... just a bit of color at a time.

Jewelry with Plastic

Jewelry created on small pieces of plastic is beautiful.

It is fun to wear... the play of opaque and transparent colors is fabulous!

Make incredible jewelry from craft plastic. Add colorful texture and embellishments right on the back of the plastic with paints and glazes. The plastic on the surface will protect the finished design.

TIP: Necklace frames are from Ranger Industries.

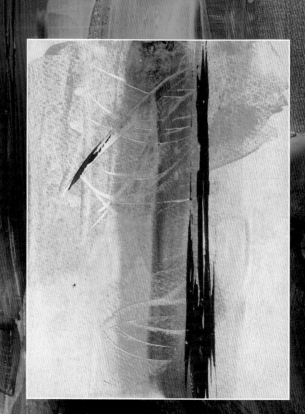

To reflect glowing light, create marks with a "color shaper" in wet glaze made with Iridescent Bright Gold.

Write marks in wet Fluid Acrylics with the point of a chopstick.

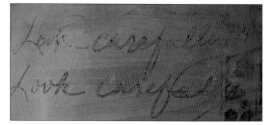

Calligraphy words into tinted Acrylic Ground for Pastels with a flat stick.

Write through wet glaze made with Copper over a Blue base.

Paint designs onto the back of a piece of plastic and allow to dry. Add the paper strip and punched hand (punched from an acrylic skin of Fiber Paste and Quinacridone Magenta) to the front of the plastic piece.

Special little metal frames make framing and mounting jewelry pendants easy. Simply secure the frame at one corner.

Making A Mark

Think of marks as letters, patterns and lines. The possibilities are endless.

Words are almost always somewhere in my work. Whether they are meaningful or gibberish, they are there. There is something both comforting and powerful about the presence of words so I use them when I can. But any kind of mark you choose to make will lend a new interest and texture to your work.

You can make your own marks on paper, canvas (don't press so hard that you tear paper or canvas), clayboard, gessoboard, plastic, acrylic or plexiglas in a number of ways. If you have nice handwriting, grab a chopstick or a toothpick and write directly into the surface of newly applied wet paint, either Fluid or Heavy Body.

As for writing with an implement directly on surfaces and dry acrylics, I find that the Sakura Gel, Glaze and Soufflé Pens work very well. I especially like the white ones!

TIP: As you scribe, clean the tip of your tool periodically to remove excess paint or product for a "cleaner" mark.

If you apply a couple of paint layers before you begin to scribe, allow them to dry and then add your "writing" paint layer, the underlying colors will be visible through your writing.

A sheer coat of an Iridescent Gold Glaze on top of color and written into is absolutely beautiful. It reflects light and makes the whole composition glow. Try it!

Writing & Mark Making In & On Hard Surfaces

Acrylics, plastic, plexiglas, clayboard and gessoboard work especially well for marking and scribing because the surface can actually be etched and scratched. This adds texture and the opportunity to rub stain into the scratches. When I have a light surface, I usually stain with a dark color and when I have a dark surface, I use a light, opaque color to stain the scratches.

Try rubbing some Micaceous Iron Oxide into the lines or words you have scribed after they are dry. It will give even more texture and interest.

Scratch into wet acrylic paint with a pointed stick or a palette knife.

Write in Iridescent colors mixed with Glazing Liquid with a flat stick.

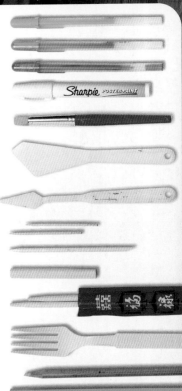

Marking tools for paper, canvas, clayboard, gesso and plastic.

Write directly into wet painted plexiglas. Allow to dry, then glaze several times for great texture and color depth.

Battery-operated etching tool is for plastic, acrylic or plexiglas only.

What You Need:
Plastic, acrylic or plexiglas
Scoring or cutting tool
for plastic
Tools and pens to make marks
Alcohol wipes to remove
oil and fingerprints

Craft plastics, acrylic and plexiglas sheets are readily available in art supply stores. They are easily cut to size using a scoring tool and a good ruler. I like the *Olfa* P-Cutter 800. Always follow directions and use a non-slip mat when using a cutting or scoring tool.

Experiment with other color combinations that will visually "mix" this way with the light. Have fun experimenting!

Acrylic Paints normally love plastics! They are in the same family after all!

Transparent pigments are the best paints to use on Plexiglas (clear) surfaces. Colors that work well are in the Quinacridone, Hansa, Phthalo and Pyrrole families along with Nickel Azo, Green Gold, Indian Yellow Hue, Manganese Blue Hue, Sap Green Hue, Permanent Violet Dark plus Transparent Yellow Iron Oxide and Transparent Red Iron Oxide.

Why these colors? Because they are transparent pigments, they are sheer enough to allow the light to pass through both the plexi and the paint, creating a "stained" glass look when the project is completed. They are wonderful in the window. Plus, when you layer the Yellow over the dried Blue, they will mix through the plexi to read as Green.

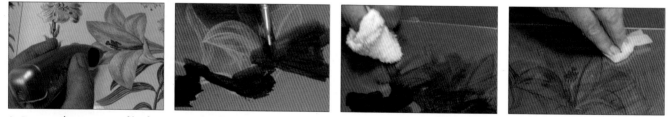

1. Remove the protective film from one side of the Plexiglas. Place the plexiglas over the copyright free image you have chosen with the exposed side facing you. Using the "Inscriblio" battery-operated engraving tool, trace over the image until fine white lines reveal the image to your satisfaction. • 2. Stain these lines by brushing a dark pigmented (Anthraquinone Blue, Jenkins Green or Dioxazine Purple) paint into them and allow it to partially dry on the surface. • 3. Rub away any excess remaining on the unscratched surface of the plexiglas with a slightly damp cloth. Try not to scrub away the paint left in the scratches. You can always repeat steps 2 & 3 if needed. • 4. Clean all remaining paint off the smooth surface using an alcohol wipe. The only paint left should now be in the scratches, revealing your design.

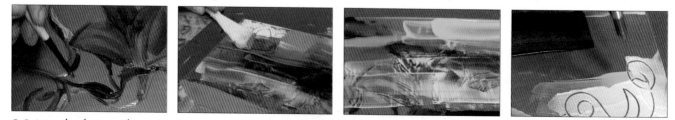

5. Paint in the design with any transparent colors you desire. Allow to dry thoroughly. • 6. With a flat, broad palette knife apply swatches of transparent pigment to the engraved side of the plexiglas in a random manner, try not to overlap wet colors. Allow to dry. • 7. Add some Interference swatches and remove some areas of paint with a color shaper for extra interest. Allow to dry. • 8. Begin to layer more paint over the dried areas, holding up the plexiglas to light to check placement. You will begin to see the color mixing occur. Complete painting on the back.

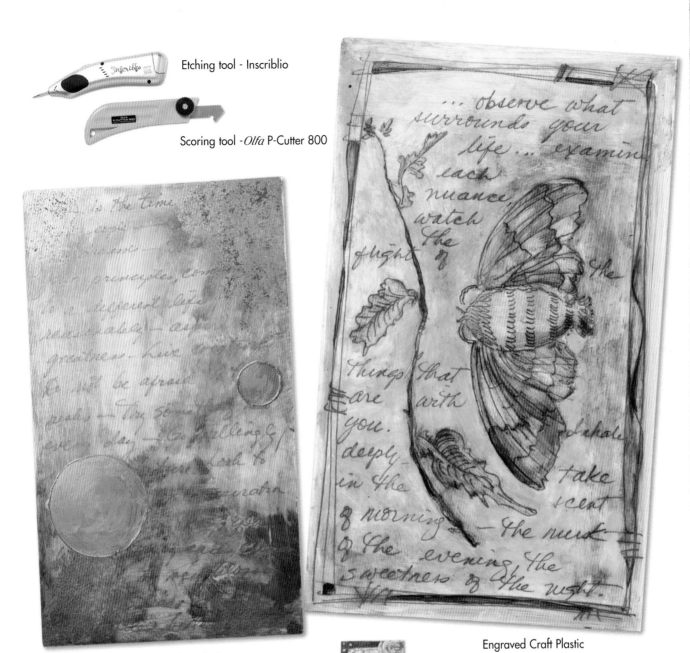

Etching tool - Inscriblio

Scoring tool - *Olfa* P-Cutter 800

Engraved Craft Plastic

Engraved Craft Plastic

Exception:

In some cases, specialty "plastics" such as HDPE (hi-density polyethylene) are used with acrylics because they <u>don't stick</u> to the paints or products. HDPE is useful for making "skins" or transfers, and for protecting surfaces as it allows you to actually peel up dried paint. HDPE is easily found as heavy duty trash bags or rolls of thick paint tarps that can be taped to your work surface or cardboard.

Add copper tape around the edges as a frame.

Begin with a small bookmark.

"Engrave" directly on white hobby plastic or clear plexiglas with an *Inscriblio* battery operated etching tool until fine white lines appear, then add paints and glazes.

Making Things Stick...
the best acrylic products for gluing this to that.

Paint with Clear Tar Gel and colors; remove paint areas with a "color shaper". The 2 round shapes are "skins" made of Fluid Acrylics. Use Soft Gel (Gloss) to adhere acrylic skins.

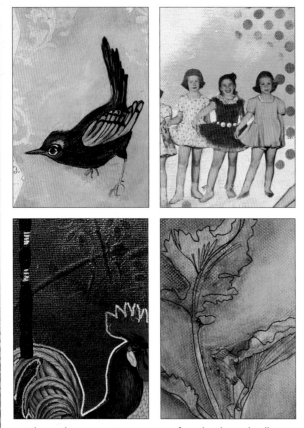

Lightweight papers, tissue, pages from books and collage papers with Polymer Medium or with a Soft Gel.

Soft Gel   Heavy Gel   Fine Pumice Gel   Molding Paste   Fluid Matte Medium

How not to become "unglued" when choosing a product for an adhesive purpose:

The need to adhere one thing to another at times is often baffling. What are the best or most effective choices to accomplish the desired result? A good "rule of thumb" is to select a product (medium, gel, or paste) whose thickness (viscosity) is similar to the thickness of the object or layer that needs to be adhered.

Lightweight papers such as tissue and pages from books do not require an extra heavy gel! To adhere papers choose instead a Polymer Medium or, better yet, a Soft Gel which is less "wet" than the mediums to adhere the layers. As the papers and objects increase in density and weight, you need to choose a product that has adequate viscosity to get the job done.

Cardboard, heavy watercolor papers, fabric, mesh or acrylic paint skins adhere well with Regular Gels. Sometimes a flat clamp or bulldog clip can help to anchor the pieces while drying.

Dimensional objects attached on assemblages or in mixed-media applications may require the Heavy or Extra Heavy Gels. These will all dry clear if the gloss variety is used, and translucent if the matte products are used. All can be tinted before application or painted after drying.

I also like to use Molding Paste, which dries to a grayish white, to adhere heavier objects to book covers or assemblages. It is easily stained or painted. While it is wet you can imbed small objects such as beads, shells and accents.

TIP: Transparencies (color or black and white) can look great in your collages, I find that it is best to use Regular Gel (Gloss) to affix them. Since transparencies don't "breathe" as paper might, it takes longer for gel to dry and you may see white areas of "wet" gel under the surface for a day or so.

I make a sandwich of a gel coat on the bottom layer that is to receive the transparency, place the transparency into the wet gel, then use a palette knife to push the surface of the transparency into the gel making sure that the gel sort of oozes out of the edges all the way around, insuring full contact with the gel.

Any gel that oozes out is just scraped across the surface of the transparency to really sandwich it to the surface. Always use Gloss Gel in this application. Matte Gels will leave a white layer that will never go away.

Adhere a watch face with Molding Paste.

Adhere a sculpted face with Molding Paste.

Adhere paper and tissue with Polymer Medium or with a Soft Gel.

Adhere dimensional flowers with Heavy Gel (Gloss).

Altered Surfaces

Aging the Page

Glazing refers to thin layers of sheer color applied over the base or underlying colors, words or images. The Glaze layer alters the underlying layers because the light goes through the colored Glaze and then bounces back off the color under it to mix in your eye.

So, by applying a sheer Blue Glaze over a Yellow undercoat, the colors mix in your eye and will read more like Green, although you didn't actually paint Green. Many of the modern colors are sheer enough to use full strength and still give a glazed effect to your work, but if you need sheerer layers, just thin your paint with Polymer Medium and you will be able to layer many fine coats without fear of being unable to see the underlying layers.

Glue a black & white transparency of a photo with Heavy Gel (Gloss), then glaze on colors. Stamp words with Iridescent Stainless Steel. Stencil dots with Light Molding Paste. Outline words and circles with Sharpie poster pens.

Images glued with Polymer Medium, then glazed with Iridescent Gold and Quinacridone Violet.

I aged this page with a glaze of Titan Buff and Naples Yellow Hue.

I painted this page with Quinacridone/Nickel Azo Gold and Sap Green Hue mixed with Titan Buff, then "aged it" with a glaze mixture of Fine Pumice Gel and Indian Yellow Hue.

You can also make "semi-transparent" or translucent glazes in at least two different ways.

Mix any mineral colors with Polymer Medium. Some that work well are the Ochres, Siennas, Umbers, along with Chromium Green, Cobalt Blue, Cobalt Teal, Ultramarine Violet with a Polymer Medium Gloss in a ratio of 5:1 medium to paint.

OR

Mix any paint with Fluid Matte Medium in the same ratio to create a soft matte finish glaze.

The examples shown on this page reflect my love of vintage family photos, the printed word (as in old pages, text and handwriting) and modern contemporary color schemes. By using glazes I am able to "see through" my bright modern colors to the vintage pages below.

When combined with other collage elements and a careful composition, the results can be delightful as well as striking.

Paynes Gray glaze

Quinacridone Burnt Orange glaze

Burnt Sienna glaze

Quinacridone/Nickel Azo Gold glaze

Titan Buff glaze

Sap Green Hue glaze

Naples Yellow Hue glaze

Burnt Umber glaze

Surface Texture: *Implied & Applied*

For the cleanest application, use a broad palette knife to push the product through the stencil going in ONE direction to prevent product from going under the stencil.

I love textures, both the kind you can see (implied) as well as the kind that you can feel (applied). It is always an adventure to figure out how to add texture to a piece I am working on. I'm going to give you a few ideas so you can start your texture adventure immediately.

Good Rule of Thumb: Almost everything that comes in a Golden white jar will give you texture. That includes the Heavy Body colors, along with gels, pastes, grounds and all their combinations.

By combinations I mean that you can mix and match products to create your own unique and personalized textures! Have fun.

Fluid Acrylics through a word stencil.

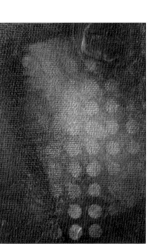

Stencil through dots with Iridescent Gold.

Heavy Body Titan Buff through a stencil.

Create a "Damask look" with a tone on tone stencil design.

Push Molding Paste through a stencil.

Push Heavy Body Interference paint through a letter stencil.

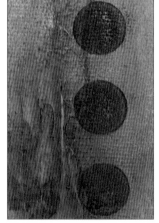

Apply Fluid Acrylic Quinacridone Red through a dot stencil.

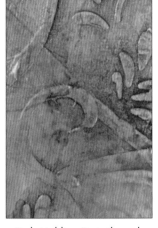

Push Molding Paste through a stencil, then stain with Airbrush colors.

Two of my favorite ways to get texture are by combining products with either stencils (the everyday plastic kind you find in your favorite Arts & Crafts stores or online) or with large foam stamps (also readily available). These are both very affordable tools which make it easy for you to get started. You should try different sponges as well for this purpose.

To make "implied" textures, use either the stencil or the stamp with paint. These give the backgrounds some variety without altering the level surface of the piece upon which you are working. You can alter the combination of colors to create tone on tone backgrounds that appear to be fabric, or use a sea sponge to create a mottled look, for example. When using the Fluid colors with a stencil, use a small amount of paint to load a common makeup sponge, pounce off the extra, and pounce the area of the stencil with the sponge to transfer the color. If you overload the sponge (usually I call this squishy), you will find that the paint oozes beneath your stencil and creates a mess. Go lightly for the best results. I also recommend using the same method to cover the back of the foam stamp with paint, rather than dipping the entire stamp into a big puddle of paint! Your results will be much cleaner and softer. You can try using the Heavy Body colors with the same application technique for slightly more texture with an almost "embossed" look to the surface.

To make "applied" textures, those that stand up and out from the surface in a physical way, you can use any of the products in the gel, paste or grounds line or any Heavy Body color (regular color, Iridescent, or Interference) and push the product through a stencil using a palette knife. You can also push a stamp or other mark maker into the product either in its natural state or after you have tinted it with color. Refer back to page 4 to see the large image on the page for some more ideas.

TIP: If you wish to use your favorite rubber stamps with Fluid Acrylics, apply the paints with a makeup sponge to the lines using a light hand and a small amount of paint.

Be sure to clean your stamp immediately to remove all traces of the paint. Be careful with your expensive rubber stamps.

Acrylic products will work best on stamps that have minimal details and lots of open space around the lines, but must be removed immediately after the image is stamped while the product is still fresh.

Stamp with transparent Fluid Acrylics on a foam stamp.

Apply several mediums - Crackle & Molding Paste, etc. then press a stamp into them.

Apply letters and scrolls through stencils with Fluid Acrylics.

Stamp with Fluid Iridescent Gold.

Stamp into Light Molding Paste, then glaze with Micaceous Iron Oxide.

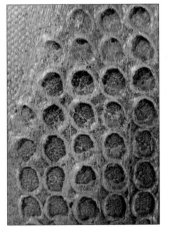

Stamp into Molding Paste, then color with Interference.

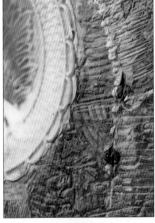

Stamp and mark textures into Molding Paste, then glaze with Fluid Acrylic colors.

Stamp into Light Molding Paste, paint with Iridescent Bronze and Iridescent Copper, then glaze with Clear Tar Gel.

Make It Matte

To understand the effect of Gloss versus Matte surfaces, think clear cellophane and wax paper.

Gloss

Matte

The image on the left is coated on the surface with Polymer Medium (Gloss). The one on the right is coated on the surface with Matte Medium (Matte).

Fluid Acrylics

Matte Fluids

The image on the above left has regular Fluid paints in transparent colors (Hansa Yellow, Quinacridone Red, Phthalo Green, Turquois Phthalo). The image on the right has the same colors in Matte Fluids.

Create a Fun Iridescent or Interference Glaze

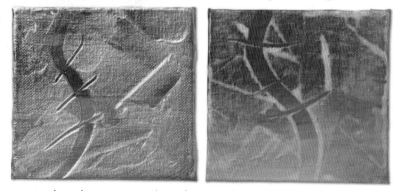

Apply a glaze mixture to the surface in a sheer or thick coat then drag a shaper, stick, stiff brush or handle through the surface to create lines and textures.

Left: Use Iridescent Silver paint mixed with Polymer Medium (Gloss). Create Magic! You will have a glowing Silver surface with lots of reflectability that partially masks the underlying color.

Right: Add Interference Violet paint to Polymer Medium (Gloss). You will create a shimmery glaze that changes in the light and interacts with the underlying color of the surface.

Polymer Medium   Matte Medium Fluid Acrylics
Matte Fluid Acrylics   Iridescent & Interference colors

Surface Sheen: More or Less

Some artist grade acrylic paints do not contain fillers or modifiers to even out the final look of the paint, so as you work you will notice a difference in the surface "glossiness" (sheen) of the various paints.

Modern pigments dry with a shiny surface (Gloss), mineral pigments dry with a flatter sheen (Matte).

So, when you use both kinds of paint in a composition, you may want to "unify" the surface sheen so you do not have areas of glossiness and flatness?

You have several options:

The first and easiest way is to put a final coat of a polymer in either Gloss or Matte over your piece as in the example shown. (two similar images with "a", one in gloss, one in matte)

Gloss will enhance the details, sharpen the color and give an overall smooth, shiny surface.

Matte will level out the surface sheen to a soft, translucent quality and diminish the "sharpness" of all the elements.

Second, you can choose to use all Matte paints. Even the modern pigments are formulated to dry with a matte surface, eliminating their natural shiny quality. Matte also imparts a more "opaque" quality to transparent pigments, making them slightly less sheer, more "dense" in appearance due to the white matting particles used in its formulation.

Third, you can add a bit of Polymer Medium (Gloss) to increase sheen in your mineral opaque colors when dried, or add a bit of matte polymer such as Matte Medium to sheer modern pigments to soften the shininess.

Or Let It Shine

Fluid Thinking–
Using Fluid Acrylics

There are so many ways to use the Fluid Acrylic colors that you will just love trying. I'm going to describe just a few here to get you excited about trying something different.

First, wet the surface of heavy watercolor paper and wash in a watered down Quinacridone Red over the wet surface. This will create areas of dark and light color depending on where the water floated the pigments on the brush.

Once that is dry, put down more Quinacridone Red straight from the container and use a diamond head palette knife to create a webby texture in the wet paint.

Allow this to dry again. Make raised circles by lifting the Cobalt Teal paint container and allowing drops to fall onto the surface. Do this with some other colors.

Don't disturb these drops and they will dry with a raised surface.

I have always loved the look of Gouache, which are really opaque watercolors. These are so easy to accomplish using Fluid Acrylics. All you need is one of my favorites … Titan Buff and the colors of your choice along with some water to loosen up the mix and allow it to be absorbed by the paper.

The opaque nature of the pigment in Titan Buff will convert even the most transparent color into an opaque tint of the same color. When washed across a piece of watercolor paper, you can achieve smoky, milky colors that are so beautifully rich!

I have a dear friend who is a talented and ardent watercolorist. Recently I have persuaded her to try Fluid Acrylics using the same watercolor techniques with which she is already so skilled.

One day in my studio, she painted this lovely little bird and was completely delighted with her results. She is now taking more serious ventures into the world of Acrylics as water media.

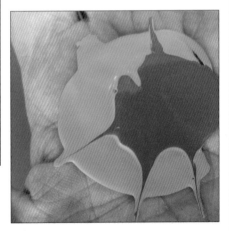

For fun one day try making some acrylic skins! Wrap a piece of cardboard with HDPE (High Density Polyethylene) and pour out a little of your favorite colors onto the board.

First squeeze out a bit of one color and use a palette knife to make it into a circle, then squeeze a second color right on top. Take a toothpick and drag some of the top color into the bottom one to make a starburst effect.

After the skin dries you can peel it up and hold it in your hand. Make lots of these little embellishments to use later.

These skins can be applied to any other acrylic background as collage elements using Soft Gel as a "glue".

One day I was inking up one of my hand-cut stamp blocks with some Titan Buff that had gotten a little too comfortable with some Interference paints left on my palette. That happy accident led me to discover an Opaque-Interference Mix. Interference paints are the sheerest paints made. So I was thrilled to see I could mix them in with the opaque Titan Buff to come up with these sort of pearly colors! Try it!

Resist Techniques
Before You Paint

A resist is basically a substance which protects a surface from receiving paints, inks or dyes - in simple terms, something that blocks the color from being absorbed into a particular area of a piece. Batik artists use wax to create a resist for the dyes used to color fabric.

Here we will use simple everyday items or other acrylic products to create resists for acrylic color.

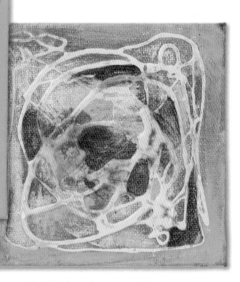

Circles: Use "removable" stickers to make a random pattern on your board or paper. Burnish down the edges before applying a coat of paint over the entire surface including the stickers. When dry, use tweezers to pull off the stickers. Enhance them with additional colors if you wish.

Doorway: Using repositionable spray adhesive, tear paper into pieces and apply to your board/paper. Then apply various colors using the paper to resist the paint. Enhance with additional paint after removing the paper.

Scribble: Clear Tar Gel loves to create strings when dripped off the end of a palette knife. Here it is applied to a white board, then allowed to dry thoroughly. Then the board is painted all over with Blue, but the area with Clear Tar Gel will "resist" the absorption of the Blue paint, which can easily be wiped off its slick surface leaving a white web.

Fence: Apply torn strips of masking tape in a random pattern on your board or paper. These areas will not receive any paint when you cover your piece with a base color. When dry, remove the tape and then use the white space for additional embellishments.

Patches: By applying random patches of Heavy Gel (Matte) to an unpainted board, you can create a resist that also has a lot of surface texture. The paint you apply can be wiped back from the gel while it is still wet to reveal a translucent stain.

Stripes: Apply White Gesso in a striped pattern onto a board or paper. This will take paint very differently than the "raw" ungessoed surface. Use this difference to your advantage!

Great results can come with drawing directly on the surface of dry acrylic paints and products.

Working on top of a ground such as Acrylic Ground for Pastels creates a surface with "tooth" that encourages pencil and pastel colors to adhere.

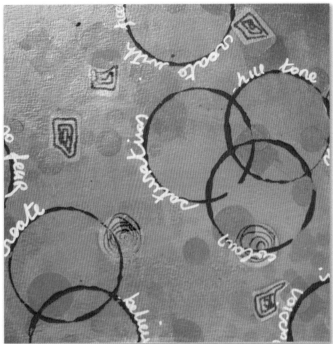

Write words directly on the surface for great embellishment.

Tint some Acrylic Ground for Pastels with Quinacridone Magenta. Apply to a board, allow to dry. Draw on the surface with pastel pencils and soft pastels.

Draw lines, squiggles and swirls with pastels, oil pastels or water-soluble pastels for a great look.

Make painterly-like drawing with poster pens. The ink "flows" out of the marker to create lines.

Note: Sharpie poster pens are "fun" embellishments for canvas, ATCs and paper arts applications, but are not recommended as fine art tools.

Let's Put Black to Work
Using Interference & Iridescent Colors

Iridescent and Interference colors are the "glitz and glimmer" of Acrylic paint! I love to demonstrate these paints as I am guaranteed "oohs and ahhs" and a few "wows" from the crowd.

Iridescent and Interference colors truly are unique, not just in appearance, but in their manufacture. These two lines of paint rely on specialized treatment of something known as "mica" to create, as in the case of the Iridescent Pigments, colors that resemble either metals or pearls, and as in the case of the Interference Acrylics, colors that do flips! Yes, flips. They look one way over white and a different way over black.

Interference colors exist naturally in nature on bird feathers, butterfly wings, and even on an oil slick. They are enchanting shifts of color that seem to change in front of our eyes depending on how the light strikes them. These colors are really exciting and can create effects that are truly "glowing."

Iridescent colors are so like the real metals they are meant to resemble, that people are always asking us if they will "oxidize" or turn Green like Copper. The answer is a resounding NO.

The "metal" paints are going to stay just as shiny and beautiful over time as they look the day you paint with them. With the exception of Iridescent Stainless Steel, Micaceous Iron Oxide and Coarse Alumina, they contain no metals at all and no "color" pigments either (except for Bronze, which has a tiny bit of Phthalo Green in it). Those little mica particles are real mimics!

Make 3 paint puddles: Interference Gold, Iridescent Gold, Cobalt Turquois.

Dab paint onto a foam stamp with a make-up sponge.

Turn the stamp over and press it onto paper or canvas.

The bar on the side of the page shows three sets of swatches of colors of Interference Acrylics over both black and white: Blue, Red & Green.

The first swatch of each color is the Interference color straight out of its container.

The second swatch is the color mixed with Iridescent Gold.

The third swatch is a mixture of the interference and a transparent Fluid color from the same "family" of colors as the interference,

and the last swatch is a mixture of the Interference, the transparent Fluid color, and the Iridescent Gold.

You can see the shifts of color that occur when these colors are blended together. The Iridescent colors are more opaque than the Interference colors so, when mixed, the blend is denser and has more visual weight.

A black background really helps to make these colors pop! When you start working with these unique paints, try them on various colored papers and see how they will change. This gives you a lot of versatility, especially with their easy mixability with all other Fluids.

Colors on the finished piece will glimmer and shimmer.

Micaceous Iron Oxide   Black Gesso

Paint Interference colors on black clayboard.
Add Glass Bead Gel and texture the Gel with a
stamp. Paint patches of Iridescent Silver.

Interference paints are the sheerest
paints made. Mix them with opaque
Titan Buff to create pearly colors!

Use Interference & Iridescent Colors on any Black Surface...
Gesso, Paint, Paper, Canvas or Board

Iridescent and Interference colors really glow when layered with Fluid Acrylics.
Even when painted over something as mundane as crinkled up deli-wrap paper,
they shimmer. The wrinkles increase the light reflection and texture.

Iridescent colors
work well on wood also.
I painted the box black to begin.

Many of us started out in art making hand-decorated cards. The search for the absolutely perfect paper to decorate the card is never-ending. With the range of colors available in Fluid Acrylics, including the Iridescent and Interference colors, your search is over. Make Your Own!

Start out with papers of varying colors (this is a good time to use the ones you don't like). Add a few drops of color, a bit of Interference, a bit of Iridescent right onto the surface of the paper. Take your trusty flat blade palette knife and drag the colors into and across each other allowing them to mix and blend before your very eyes.

You will soon learn that letting some of the background color peek through really enhances the look of the hand-decorated papers. All you need are a few details added with a Poster Paint Pen or a Jelly Roll Pen and you are on your way.

Another fun technique is to add foam stamped images using Interference colors onto black paper. Or try stencils in an overall pattern. You can even make textured paper by pushing a thin layer of tinted Molding Paste through a stencil and getting a raised embossed surface! The ideas are endless. Give it a try.

If you love the look of iridescents, try creating your own using combinations of the Iridescent and Interference colors. Whether you use white, black or colored paper as the base, these paints will always add the perfect touch.

Use Interference & Iridescent Colors on any Surface... Paper, Canvas or Board

They are ever changing and will surprise you each and every time.

Set the stage for wonderful handmade cards with glossy and shimmering Interference and Iridescent colors. Make handmade papers beforehand to use as collage elements, or add colors directly on the surface of the card.

Background Basics *and Creating Depth of Field through Color and Black*

Backgrounds on Black

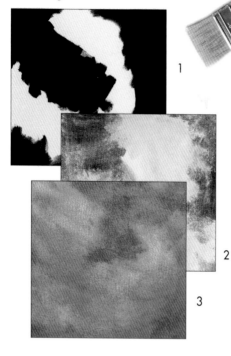

1

2

3

Black Gesso
covers in one coat

"Black"ground Basics: Building a color rich background

I have found that in order to achieve a highly luminous base to receive my color choices it is better if I add some black areas to my white canvas or paper. The first time I teach this technique to any group of students I always expect them to get up and walk out! But it Always works and the results are worth the tiny bit of anxiety that must be experienced whenever you put that first black mark on your white background.

Just remember, rich color backgrounds are important beginnings to a great final outcome. When I'm composing a piece, I consider the color family that either relates to or complements any collage element I may want to use. This will help me choose the opaque and transparent paint colors to add to the Black, Titan Buff and Titanium White patches I put on every piece.

Black serves to create a depth in the background that I haven't been able to achieve in other ways. On these pages I went through the process of creating the background both with the black applied and without. You will be able to see the difference for yourself. Try it both ways; the results of the layered effect are outstanding.

Steps for Great "Black"grounds

1. Paint canvas board, paper with Black Gesso. Let dry.
2. Add areas of Titan Buff and Titanium White overlapping and exposing some of the Black to create areas of high color contrast. Use a "dry brush" technique.
3. Add an opaque paint color in same way as #2, repeat with second opaque in same color family; I used the "Yellow-Orange" family and started with Yellow Ochre, and Naples Yellow Hue.
4. Add a transparent paint color in the same way, then a second transparent paint color; I used Indian Yellow Hue, Nickel Azo Yellow, then added Quinacridone/Nickel Azo Gold, Quinacridone Magenta, and Quinacridone Burnt Orange. You can continue adding as many transparent colors as you wish at this stage. Use very little paint and make the layers very thin. It is not necessary to put each color over every square inch… hit and miss is better!
5. Add color details. Here I used a stencil to make the large Turquoise circles out of a tint I mixed - Turquois Phthalo & Titan Buff with a bit of Phthalo Green (Blue Shade).
6. Add collage element - adhere with Soft Gel (Gloss).
7. HUMMINGBIRD on page 27: Add the texture details when collage elements are dry (here I used a mix of Fine Garnet Gel with Iridescent Copper and stamped it on using a wooden ruler to which I had applied the paint mixture.)

Backgrounds on White & Buff

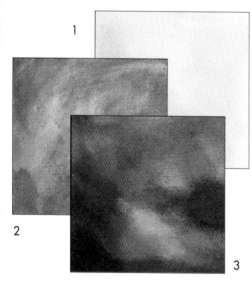

1

2

3

Try this color combo: Cobalt Blue, Cerulean Blue Chromium, Phthalo Blue (Red Shade), Anthraquinone Blue, Manganese Blue Hue.

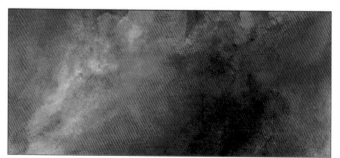

Try this color combo: Quinacridone Red, Transparent Pyrrole Orange, Nickel Azo Yellow.

Try These Ideas

TIP: Don't think too much about where you put the first black splotch - just do it. Let it dry, and then add the Titan Buff, let dry, then the white. Let them touch; let them overlap thinly in places.

This is a random process. Do several small canvases or boards at one time, then you'll be all set for future color choices when you are ready.

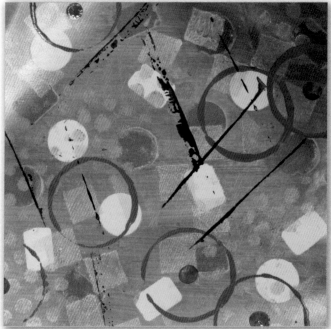

Multiple layers of color create a mystical and unusual background. Stamp simple shapes on top with unusual brilliant colors.

Try this color combo: Chromium Oxide Green, Phthalo Green (Yellow Shade), Turquois Phthalo, Green Gold.

Mediums & Gels – A Coat of Many Options

A medium is a polymer product that is more fluid in consistency than a gel, which is thicker and more like a paste. We use the term Viscosity to refer to this thickness or thinness of products in the Acrylic line.

Not only do the polymer mediums and gels come in various viscosities, they also come in a number of surface sheens ranging from Gloss (shiny) to Semi-Gloss (less shiny, a bit translucent, eggshell finish), to Matte (flat and almost opaque).

The three canvases shown here demonstrate these surface sheens and how they show as glazes (swirls) and how they mix with color and the addition of another product. The bottom left-hand corner of each one shows the Gel in its untinted state.

For specialty gels and their applications see pages 43 - 45.

What does a medium or gel do?

1. Gloss: Soft Gel (Gloss) and Fluid Quinacridone Magenta were mixed together to make the glaze which was combed after it was applied. It is easy to see the surface shine on the edges of the swirls. Glass beads were then added to the Magenta glaze and applied in the bottom right corner of the canvas. They further increase the reflectivity on the surface.

2. Semi-Gloss: Soft Gel (Semi-Gloss) was used to make the glaze. There is somewhat less shine and a softer reflectivity coming from the surface. I added Interference Violet to the Magenta glaze and applied it with a palette knife to the bottom right-hand corner. It shows a soft translucent effect.

TIP: Keep a written record of your experimental "combinations" so that you will have a formula to return to if you like the results, and a record of what didn't work!

The thicker, more viscous gels produce more surface textures. They hold marks and writing, allowing you to score and draw into them while still holding their shape.

Experiment with unexpected tools.

3. Matte: Soft Gel (Matte) was used for the glaze on this canvas. The swirls are much more opaque and the surface is very flat. Iridescent Gold paint was mixed with the glaze to create a Pinkish–Gold area on the bottom right, which is totally opaque.

Choose your products giving thought to the surface sheen you ultimately want to see. It is best not to use a Matte Gel over images as it will reduce your ability to see the details. All matte products contain "white" particles which cloud the clear polymer gel and create a flatter, more opaque surface.

Because gels have various thicknesses (viscosities), they may accumulate too much white and block out what you may have wanted to see. When assembling a collage, use gloss products to adhere all the layers. If at the end you want a "matte" surface sheen, then use Fluid Matte Medium (very thin and not viscous) as a fine coat over the entire surface.

All mediums and gels can be mixed with paints to create colored glazes that vary in viscosity and range from sheer to opaque. You can also mix these gels with other products to create textural variations. Remember that this is a mix and match system, so make lots of combinations to discover the potential available to you.

Totally Encaustic

or Maximum Matte

If you have an interest in the look of "beeswax" or encaustic painting but are hesitant because of the heat involved or feel it might be too complicated, here is an acrylic version that is an effective visual substitute for the real thing.

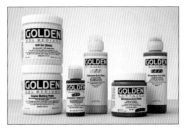

Soft Gel (Matte)
Interference and Iridescent Colors

Encaustic Glaze Formula

3 heaping Tablespoons of Soft Gel (Matte)
5 drops Iridescent Gold
5 drops Interference Blue
1 drop Quinacridone/ Nickel Azo Gold

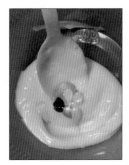

Mix thoroughly, but do not beat.

Optional: Add a bit of water to loosen the mixture.

More Ideas:

Try using a base of Molding Paste and setting objects into it. Allow to dry, then use encaustic glaze.

"Imbed" objects (such as shells) into a layer of Molding Paste. Paint the entire surface with Titan Buff, including the objects. Apply glaze stain with sheer color.

Actually bury things into the glaze such as the keys, threads and accents.

Tip: Rub a bit of Micaceous Iron Oxide into the surface when completely dry to age it.

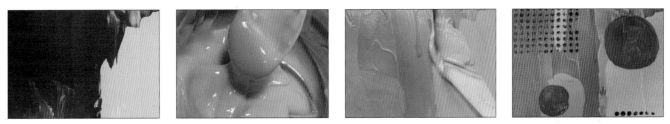

1. Paint your rigid surface (in this case an Ampersand Cradle Board with strong bright colors which will be able to stand out under the acrylic "beeswax" glaze that will be applied. I chose Pyrrole Red, Naples Yellow Hue and Cobalt Teal. Allow to dry. • 2. Mix the Encaustic Glaze formula above. • 3. Apply one coat of the "faux-encaustic" glaze to cover the entire surface. Allow to dry completely. • 4. Add color details on top of the glaze layer. Here I added two Blue circles, and some stamped dots. Allow to dry thoroughly.

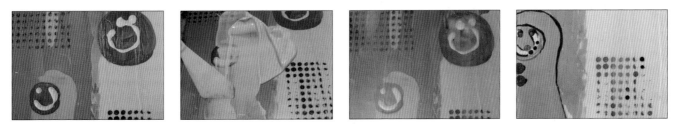

5. Add some "details" by squeezing paint directly from the Fluid Acrylic container to produce a "raised" line. Here I used Yellow to begin creating details. Allow to dry. • 6. Add the second coat of the "faux-encaustic" glaze to cover entire surface. • 7. Allow to dry completely. • 8. Optional: Add details on top of the glaze for a pop of color and contrast with the underlying muted layers.

Pastes & Grounds

Regular Molding Paste is one of my favorite products. There is something very wonderful about the smooth, cool surface which takes paint, stains, and glazes with such versatility.

Regular Molding Paste is actually made with marble dust which contributes to its almost porcelain-like surface, which is slightly slick and not absorbent.

Molding Paste has the ability to hold various lines, textures, and patterns, making it able to mimic all sorts of interesting surfaces, from Tiffany glass, to heat patinated copper. Very thick applications can become quite heavy, so consider this when choosing what you will apply the paste upon.

Molding Paste
Crackle Paste   Coarse Molding Paste
Light Molding Paste   Fiber Paste

Provencal Fabric - Deconstructed: I used muted (mineral) colors to paint a background, mostly in Greens and Golds. Then I added a raised pattern to the painted surface by pushing Molding Paste through a variety of stencils, allowing it to dry before adding more color. I added a couple of collage elements then buried it under a coat of Clear Tar Gel for a shiny surface and to soften the edges. My final touch was applying the Cobalt Teal circles with stencils and biscuit cutters.

Hearts Painting: After dividing the canvas into quadrants and painting each in different shades of Quinacridone Reds and Violets, I pushed Molding Paste through a stencil cut from a foam food packing tray. Next I glazed the surface with Interference and Iridescent Paints using the burnishing technique on page 33.

Textures Galore:

Texture can be so exciting ... that is what makes this blue beauty one of my favorite pieces!

Try mixing and matching various Pastes and Gels on a surface.

Push Light Molding Paste through a stencil.

Push a mixture of Coarse Pumice Gel through a stencil, then wash a mixture of Garnet Gel and Iridescent Copper on top.

Add an area of Crackle Paste. When dry, apply a wet wash of Iridescent Bronze and watch the Green pigment float down into the cracks, leaving the Bronze mica chips on the surface.

Mix Pumice Gel with Turquois Phthalo to make a texture.

Mix Pumice Gel with Micaceous Iron Oxide, Garnet Gel and Iridescent Copper to make a thick glaze.

Application Ideas

Pastes are texture friendly products which give an incredible range of options to achieve different looks. They are all opaque, drying various shades of white or near white. The pastes introduced on the next pages are various kinds of Molding Pastes, Crackle Paste, and Fiber Paste.

Each paste has its own unique set of properties which you will discover as you apply them. Pastes can all be used directly from their containers, or mixed with paints to provide color.

Keep in mind that because they are white, they will mix with color as tints or pastels. You can tint almost any paste to achieve strong color or apply them straight from their containers and apply color after they dry (or even while still wet).

Gels have "built in" texture created by particles (glass beads, garnet pieces or pumice). The tiny particles are suspended in a gel medium which make textures when dried.

Because gels dry clear, you can change the color of them dramatically by adding paint. It really alters the appearance of the particles in a surprising manner.

Grounds are products that alter the surface of your art to allow you to write or draw upon it. They have a very slight texture that is often described as "gritty" or as "having tooth". If you like to work in pastels or color pencil these are exciting options.

If you just like to experiment with various looks, I find their subtle texture and the way in which they take color very compelling.

They also happen to be excellent for making transfers! The possibilities are truly endless. Your texture adventure is about to begin.

Have fun experimenting! Add a mixture of Coarse Alumina with Interference Blue. Draw the circles with pastel pencils. Add an Iridescent Silver stripe.

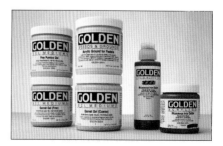

Fine Pumice Gel   Acrylic Ground for Pastels
Garnet Gel (Fine)   Regular Gel (Gloss)
Micaceous Iron Oxide

Molding Paste

Burnished Green Circles: I made these fun circle shapes with graduated biscuit cutters pushed into wet Molding Paste. When dry, I painted them with Iridescent and Interference colors.

Wild Fire Painting:

I applied Molding Paste with a broad flat palette knife to an Ampersand Cradle Board. I covered most of the board, leaving only a small area of surface without paste. I left areas of definite texture on the surface for effect and made small pinholes with a toothpick.

I let the piece dry thoroughly, then added paint to highlight the textured areas.

As a final embellishment, I applied a "Skin" of Iridescent Copper paint on the surface using Soft Gel to adhere it.

Magical Molding Pastes

The Great Mimics

Molding Paste is designed to create texture and hardness. It is one of my favorite mediums. I love to comb and stamp textures into the wet surface. It works best when applied with an old credit card or a flat blade palette knife.

Experiment by using thinned Fluid Acrylics in a watercolor fashion or Heavy Body Acrylics applied thickly. Glaze over the texture. This will allow the paint to gather in the deep crevices created by the application of Molding Paste with a palette knife.

How to Burnish the Surface
and layer or Remove Colors on Molding Paste

Burnishing Technique on Molding Paste:

By varying the color combinations used in this technique you can produce a wide range of "mock" surfaces: wood grain, copper flashing, verdigris copper, Tiffany glass, etc.

TIP: Molding Paste can lend itself to a variety of textures depending on how it is applied. Large flat strokes will give you a surface that mimics wood planks complete with knots. Short flat strokes placed randomly can create mountain ranges in a landscape painting. You can apply it as if you are plastering a wall for a great antique look, or lift the flat face of a palette knife up and down in the wet paste to create a web.

This one looks like wood grain, aged teak, I think!

Color combination:
Cerulean Blue Chromium, Quinacridone Burnt Orange, Interference Oxide Green

1. To a surface of dry Molding Paste which has been applied with a palette knife, generously apply a strong opaque color (here I used Cerulean Blue Chromium) with a flat brush. • 2. When the paint has barely dried, take the corner of a terry cloth rag and wipe away the excess paint leaving the Molding Paste "stained" the color of the paint applied. • 3. Apply a contrasting color on some areas using a sheer pigment (I used Quinacridone Burnt Orange) in the same manner as before, wiping it off almost immediately, but not completely. The color will settle in the grooves left from the applicator (palette knife, or spackle knife).

Acrylic Glazing Liquid (Gloss)
Acrylic Glazing Liquid (Satin)
Molding Paste
Heavy Body Acrylic colors

4. The third color application should be an Interference Oxide (Green, in this case) color which complements the color choices made so far. Paint over the entire surface, and then remove in the same manner as before. • 5. The final application is an Iridescent color (Bronze in this case). Apply generously to the entire surface, and allow to dry almost completely. • 6. Then apply a squirt of Acrylic Glazing Liquid (Satin) to the cloth and start to buff away some of the layers of paint, exposing the underlying layers as desired. The best effects are achieved by doing this unevenly and revealing the various colors. You can always add more color and take it off again. The Acrylic Glazing Liquid acts as an "eraser" of sorts in this application.

Additional color combinations:
Using Cobalt Teal, Turquois Phthalo, Iridescent Gold, Interference Green

Using Quinacridone Burnt Orange, Indian Yellow Hue, Iridescent Copper, Interference Orange

Using Chromium Oxide Green, Green Gold, Interference Green, Iridescent Gold

Light Molding Paste

Light Molding Paste has been formulated to be much lighter, more than 50% lighter, than regular Molding Paste. It actually reminds me of "marshmallow creme" when I spoon it out of the jar! It is very fluffy, dries to a brilliant white (I recommend it for use as a white) and has an amazing surface that behaves like a very absorbent watercolor paper.

Wet the dried Light Molding Paste surface with plain water before adding paint and watch the colors literally explode on the surface pulling down and through the paste! It is like fireworks!

You can mop up excess wet paint off the surface with a towel or rag, leaving only what you want to stay, and then add more colors with the same absorbency.

Light Molding Paste

Light Molding Paste dries to a flat, matte surface which remains quite absorbent unless sealed. You can add color, allow the color to dry, then rewet the surface and add other colors without disturbing the first set. The trick is to let each set of colors dry thoroughly in between so they are locked in.

Since it dries to a flat paper-like sheen, you can make it glossy by adding a coat of a gloss medium, or a high gloss product like Clear Tar Gel or Self Leveling Clear Gel.

Washes of vibrant, transparent color (Phthalo Blue, Quinacridone Magenta, Phthalo Green) applied on a dry Light Molding Paste surface that has been partially wet, allowed to dry, then rewet adding additional colors and some Iridescent Gold.

You can apply paint in several ways:

With a wet brush on a wet surface, or with a dry brush on a wet surface, or with a wet brush on a dry surface, or with a dry brush on a dry surface … each time it will be different! So be sure to try it out every way so you can enjoy Light Molding Paste to its fullest.

Try a variety of foam stamps.

Experiment with imprinting foam stamps and other tools into Light Molding Paste. It is also a great surface for marking into while wet.

The furrows and designs left behind after the paste has dried leave great places for color to

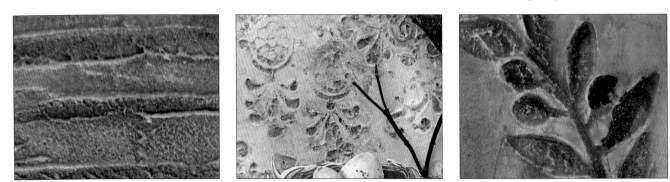

Make impressions by using foam stamps pressed into wet paste, remove immediately. Let dry. Paint the surface as desired to give various effects.

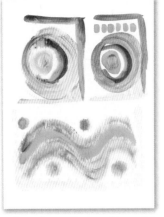

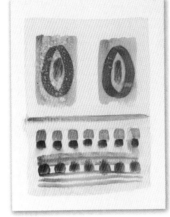

Absorbent Ground is useful for creating washes and stains with acrylic and watercolor paints. Apply with a brush, roller or squeegee.

Absorbent Ground creates an absorbent surface similar to watercolor paper. It can be tinted with a few drops of Fluid Acrylics. (Varnishing is recommended.)

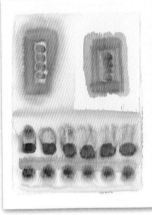

Acrylic Ground for Pastels creates a great "tooth" for pencils, crayons, pastels and water media. Here I applied Fluid Acrylics.

Acrylic Ground for Pastels (tinted with Quinacridone/Nickel Azo Gold) creates a great "tooth" for pencils, crayons, pastels and water media.

Many watercolor enthusiasts use Fluid Acrylics to lay down permanent washes that won't lift by thinning paints down with water to a watery consistency.

You can create wonderful and unusual textures and surfaces with "Grounds" on paper or canvas. Experiment with different Grounds for painting ... Light Molding Paste, Absorbent Ground and Acrylic Ground for Pastels. Add watercolor or Fluid Acrylics on top.

Textured Egg: Add texture to Fluid Acrylics used as watercolors with textured gels. Here Garnet Gel was applied to an egg shape for the rusty spots found in robin eggs. For color, a Fluid Acrylic wash was applied after the gel dried.

Experiment with Fluid Acrylics as Water Media!

Crackle Effects

Crackle Paste is a unique product that actually forms cracks as it dries. The size of the cracks depend on how thinly (fine and small cracks) or thickly (large and deep cracks) this white, opaque paste is applied. You should get a good crackle when your application film is at least 1/8" thick.

There are three important things to know about *Crackle Paste:*

1. It needs a rigid surface for best effect, so try it on canvas boards, Ampersand boards, or paper that has been glued to a board.
2. It likes to take its time to dry … it really cannot be rushed by using a hair dryer or heat gun. If you force-dry it, don't expect cracks to show up!
3. If you wish to add some color to this paste while it is wet, use no more than 10 percent paint. Crackle Paste is fragile and temperamental in this situation.

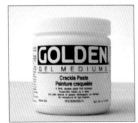

Crackle Paste

Clayboard and Gessoboard are rigid surfaces, perfect for Crackle Paste.

Painted Pear - Crackle Paste makes a great surface upon which to do traditional water media effects since it behaves like watercolor paper, only with cracks in it. Water media pear by Sally Markell of Memphis, Tennessee.

"Majolica" Mimic - When wet, you can stamp into Crackle Paste with foam stamps, just as with the other pastes.

 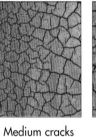 

Small cracks   Medium cracks   Large cracks

The thickness of the applied coat = the size of the cracks.
Applied in a thin coat, it produces small cracks.
Applied in a medium thick coat, it produces medium cracks.
Applied in a thick coat, it produces large cracks.

Crackle Paste can be easily applied with a wide palette knife, an old credit card or a painter's squeegee.

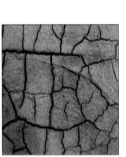

Experiment by flowing different colors into the cracks.

Crackle Paste may be a bit "fussy" about a few details, but the beauty of its application is worth the small accommodations we must make! It takes color so beautifully and with interesting variations due to the way the pigments from the paint settle into the cracks and deepen in tone.

Wet the dry surface, then add the color of your choice and watch the paint seep and travel through the cracked surface. Add additional colors and they will blend.

Stencil a "Dirty Glaze" on top of cracked texture for an antique look - see page 41.

Fiber Paste...
Fibers for Texture

Suspended in Fiber Paste are fibers that create a wonderful texture when spread onto a surface. They dry to resemble hand-made deckle-edged paper.

Fiber Paste dries bright white straight from the jar, but can also be very easily colored while still wet by mixing in a few drops of Fluid Acrylics. The colored paste then dries to resemble colored paper. It makes great "skins" with definite deckling on the edges!

Apply Fiber Paste with a flat, broad palette knife. After it is on the area you desire, wet the knife and draw its edge over the wet paste to smooth it down and remove any edges.

Fiber Paste is sturdy enough to "capture" or imbed an object. Put on a thick coat and push a flat-backed object into it. Wait until dry, then add paint and color.

The texture really shows when finished with Iridescent and Interference colors.

Fiber Paste

TIP: To get a clean, hard edge which will make the Fiber Paste look like a blocked paper and not deckled, use a low-stick masking tape to block out the area where you wish to apply the paste. Apply the paste as thick as you wish, then immediately pull up the tape and allow the paste to dry thoroughly.

Voila - Straight, thick edges of "paper!"

TIP: One last thought - Since Fiber Paste most mimics paper, this is a great product to "draw" on with your colored pencils after it is dry. Try it, it's fun to play on.

On the dry surface use a wet brush and apply Fluid Acrylics. This will allow the paint to be absorbed only into the very top layers of the paste and the color will be more patchy. Once dried, you can rewet and fill in the patchy areas with another color of your choice.

This collage was first prepared by painting a canvas board with a pastel tint made from Manganese Blue Hue and Titanium White. Skins were made from both plain and tinted Fiber Paste on an HDPE surface. See how the deckle edge on the white skin looks like handmade paper. Some skins were scraped through while wet, leaving striped areas that are actually openings in the skin.

The skins were applied to the Blue board using Soft Gel (Matte). When everything was dry, I added additional collage elements, stenciled areas and hand-painted dots to complete the piece.

Coarse Molding Paste was first applied to the Ampersand Cradle board and painted while it was wet with Cerulean Blue, creating a bumpy texture where the brush strokes mixed the paint and paste together.

When it was totally dry, an additional wash of Cerulean Blue was added to even out the color. Areas of Green and Yellow in leaf shapes were then added and allowed to dry.

I scraped across the rough surface of the piece with a palette knife dipped into Naphthol Red Fluid Acrylics and then again with Titanium White.

The lines were added at the end to define the leaf areas.

Coarse Molding Paste...
with a Gritty Surface

The entire line of Molding Pastes is really exciting and each one has its own characteristics.

Coarse Molding Paste has some interesting qualities: it dries white like all the others, but it is a bit more translucent and it also has a somewhat grainy, gritty surface upon drying.

It can be painted directly into with Fluid Colors while wet leaving behind an interesting pattern of brush strokes that are a mix of the paste and paints. Try applying a smooth level coat onto a surface, allowing it to dry completely. Then wet the surface, adding both Fluid Acrylics and Airbrush colors. The two looks are totally different, yet highly appealing visually.

Once dry, paste can be painted in several ways:

Wet it first, then add in Fluid Acrylics with a very wet brush. You will see the paints flow through the film to give a rich and vibrant color to the paste.

I have also found the Airbrush colors to be amazingly effective on this product.

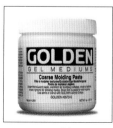

Coarse Molding Paste

Airbrush colors create glowing colors and are amazingly effective on Fiber Paste and on Coarse Molding Paste.

Mix Coarse Pumice Gel and Molding Paste, then apply to the surface of a board. Add wonderful colors with Fluid Acrylics and Water-Soluble Oil Pastels.

Micaceous
Iron Oxide

Coarse
Alumina

Acrylic Ground
for Pastels

Iridescent
Stainless Steel

Micaceous Iron Oxide can be written and drawn upon with any soft "lead" or chalk/crayon implements, and is especially effective with water-soluble oil pastels.

Gritty – Toothy Surfaces

with Grounds and other Products

There are many acrylic products available that have a gritty quality to them that is often called "tooth". It is this quality that gives you the ability to actually "write" or mark on them with a wide variety of materials such as chalk, pastels, pastel pencils, oil pastels, colored pencils, and graphite pencils.

The "tooth" grabs the soft particles of these various materials and holds them to the surface. Draw words, shapes or circles using pastel pencils.

Some of the products in this category are actually called "grounds" and others behave in the same way, but don't carry the word "ground" on their label.

Coarse Alumina has similar properties to Micaceous Iron Oxide, but with a chunkier texture and larger grit. It mixes well with color to achieve a dense and grainy background. I love to use it in combination with one or more of the Iridescent paints, especially Silver and Stainless Steel.

Acrylic Ground for Pastels is great for anyone who loves the soft quality of "sanded" paper. Apply it to your paper or board and make marks on it. Use it plain or tint it any color you wish. It takes color beautifully with a slightly translucent, alabaster-like, quality. As a surface for paint it is really wonderful as it takes color more like a stain, but still allows you to see through it somewhat to what you have placed underneath.

Altered Surfaces

How to Mix a "Dirty Glaze"

Sometimes things just look a bit too new or clean for me. I like interest and depth to my surfaces. This quick and easy glaze turned out to be just the trick to solve the problem!

Start with 8 parts Polymer Medium (Gloss or Matte, your choice) and 1 part Micaceous Iron Oxide. If you wish to color the glaze slightly, add one drop Fluid color of your choice to the mix. Mix thoroughly using a palette knife.

1. Mix 8 parts polymer medium (gloss or matte) and 1 part Micaceous Iron Oxide.

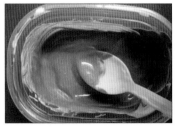

2. Mix thoroughly.

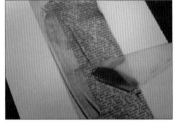

3. Apply dirty glaze to surface using palette knife or brush.

4. Uneven strokes will give you lighter and darker areas of glaze when dried.

How to Mix a Gritty Dirty Glaze

The "tooth" grabs the soft particles of these various materials and holds them to the surface. I used pastel pencils to draw in the circles on the side of this canvas.

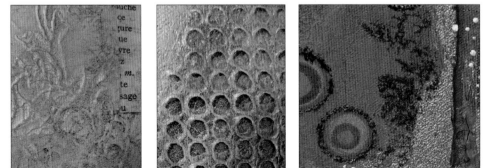

Micaceous Iron Oxide

Micaceous Iron Oxide is a sparkling, nearly black, paint product with a fine grit which really grabs hold of any number of writing products. It can be tinted with paint to take on various shades of color while retaining its dark and twinkling surface. It is one of my very favorite products and I use it in many different ways.

Micaceous Iron Oxide makes a great "dirty" glaze. I rub it into the crevices of textured surfaces for added interest. I push it through stencils for a "flocked" effect.

The surface can be written upon with any soft "lead" or chalk/crayon implements, and is especially effective with water-soluble oil pastels. Use it as a shadow in a still-life painting or use it for a gray in a value study. It is really versatile and fun to use.

TIP: Apply a "dirty glaze" over the surface to cover words, paper, canvas and images, and to add a slightly dirty, gritty layer. This glaze can also be pushed through a stencil for a subtle pattern.

TIP: Apply a "dirty glaze" thinly for an even glaze, apply generously and unevenly for a more textured glaze with areas of more and less grit. Allow the "dirty glaze" to sink into textured areas.

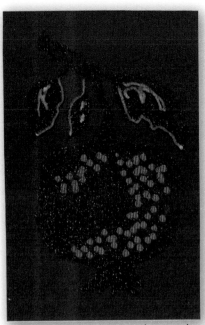

Apply Micaceous Iron Oxide to a rubber stamp, then stamp the image on your surface for an interesting effect.

Fine Pumice Gel

Pumice Gel comes in several textures, but for use as a ground, the Fine grade is most effective.

Fine Pumice dries with a somewhat translucent quality to its surface and tends towards a slightly gray finish. Coarser grades have a very gray appearance in the jar and when used untinted.

Pumice takes to color unbelievably well and by adding a few drops of Fluid Color you can change the character of the gray pumice completely.

Fine Pumice Gel

All Pumice Gels are highly absorbent when dry. By first wetting the surface, you can add layers of color onto a surface coated with pumice quite easily. I love using water-soluble oil pastels on top of Coarse Molding Paste to enhance details.

Try layering other gels over the top of Pumice Gel for some interesting effects. My favorite is Molding Paste with Coarse Pumice.

1. Cover surface using Fine Pumice mixed with a few drops of Fluid Sap Green Hue. Allow to dry. • 2. Add an area of Light Molding Paste in the center of the surface. Push in a foam stamp to create texture while paste is still wet. Allow to dry. • 3. Wet the surface of the dried paste and tint it with a wash of Quinacridone Magenta mixed with Titan Buff and water. Blot off excess paint, leaving more color to sit in crevices. Allow to dry. • 4. Highlight areas with Fluid Acrylics of your choice. • 5. Add collage elements.

Tip: Blending on the Surface

Apply a layer of Coarse Molding Paste to a surface. Paint into the paste while wet using Fluid Manganese Blue Hue, creating a textured surface. Allow to dry thoroughly.

Apply an area of Fine Pumice Gel in the center of the piece. Allow to dry. Paint Pumice with a wash of Quinacridone Magenta and Titan Buff thinned with water. Allow to dry.

Paint in a botanical image of leaves with Fluid Sap Green Hue thinned with Polymer Medium.

Leaves painted by Sally Markell, Memphis, Tennessee

Glittering Glass Beads

Imagine being able to capture all the sparkle of a crystal chandelier in a paint film! In Glass Bead Gel thousands of tiny clear glass beads are suspended in a gel medium that will lay flat against any surface after you apply it with a palette knife.

Once the white wet gel has dried and turns clear, the beads captured in the clear film begin to sparkle. But, even better yet, try tinting your Glass Bead Gel with the transparent color of your choice. Try Quinacridone Magenta or Turquois Phthalo.

Consider tinting this gel with an Interference Color for a surprising boost in reflectability! Enjoy the possibilities.

Make a Milk Glass Transfer

Glass Bead Transfer...

1. Gesso the center of a small piece of frayed canvas (add color if desired), allow to dry.

2. Coat gessoed area with a thin coat of Coarse Molding Paste, allow to dry.

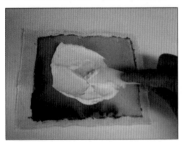

3. Wet the Coarse Molding Paste with water and apply wash of a sheer pigment, in this case Phthalo Blue (Red Shade), allow to dry.

4. Apply Glass Bead Gel directly from the container onto the painted area going beyond where you wish to place your transfer.

5. Place a toner-based copy of an image face down into the glass beads and gently rub the surface with your fingers to make sure that all the surface of the paper is in direct contact with the wet Glass Bead Gel. Allow to dry completely.

6. Wet the back of the transfer paper with a bit of water using your fingers to push it all over the surface. You will see the paper turn gray as it absorbs the water. Wait a moment or so and then start rubbing the paper away from the surface with your thumb. A slightly damp sponge also works well. Keep rubbing away the pulp until the transfer image is completely visible and has no white film showing (this is just more pulp, so keep working until it is gone). Your image will appear frosty due to the glass beads.

I highlighted the glass beads that remained uncovered by the transfer with Green and Blue Interference Colors mixed with Turquois Phthalo. These remained very sparkly and the color really enhanced their effect.

Here Glass Bead Gel is used as a transfer medium under an image ... very effective in a surprising way.

When ink is transferred onto Glass Bead Gel, that area becomes "frosty", with all the surrounding areas outside of the transfer remaining sparkling!

Glass Bead Gel also creates a wonderful texture and sparkle when applied over images. For this collage I applied tinted Fiber Paste and stamped a small texture in the wet surface. After it dried I used Fluid Acrylics as a water media. As the final touch I added a layer of Glass Bead Gel.

This image shows how Glass Bead Gel can be used in a "mixed-media" collage over Fiber Paste and various colors!

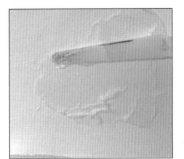

Glass Bead Gel

Clear Tar Gel

Through the Looking Glass
Slick, Shiny, Stringy
and Self Leveling

Clear Tar Gel and Self Leveling Clear Gel are the "crystals" of the gel world. They have unique properties that set them apart from regular gels and mediums.

Both are pourable with self-leveling properties. This means that although you may use a palette knife to apply these products, the strokes of the knife will disappear as the product relaxes and finds its level.

Be sure to work on a "flat" surface or you could find these gels sliding right off the table!

Another great thing about these two products is their crystal-clear clarity! Although they are very white when wet, they are truly see-through when dry and produce a wonderful shiny surface on projects when you want a shiny look with a highly smooth surface.

This clarity visually enhances and sharpens the underlying colors as well! If you have a piece with a lot of surface texture, a coat of one of these gels will push the texture back and bury it in a glassy layer. It is quite beautiful.

You will notice that both of these products are quite "viscous" but in a different way than the gel line. In this case the Clear Tar Gel's viscosity translates to a stringy quality which is wonderful to drip off the end of a palette knife, creating fine threads which will act as a clear resist over whatever is underneath it.

Clear Tar Gel and Self Leveling Clear Gel can be colored with Fluid Acrylics, but give them time to rest after mixing in the color so that any air bubbles that might have formed can rise to the surface and pop. If you have air bubbles visible in these gels after you have spread them out, just take a toothpick and pop them in the wet product. They will go away!

Add Clear Tar Gel for a high gloss surface.

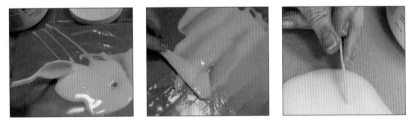

Making A "Skin": 1. Pour out Self Leveling or Clear Tar Gel onto a board covered in a thick plastic trash bag or a Non-Stick Craft Sheet (*Ranger Industries*). • 2. Spread with palette knife to an even layer. • 3. Use a toothpick to pop any air bubbles that may appear.

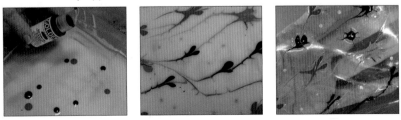

4. Immediately drop Fluid Acrylics here and there through the film. Use 3-5 colors that you like. • 5. Draw through the colors with a toothpick, creating patterns similar to marbled paper. Allow to dry until completely clear. • 6. Peel off the HDPE and cut into shapes to use as collage elements.

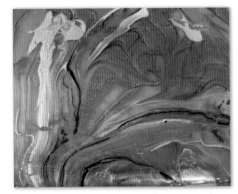

Variation: Pour a layer of one of the gels over an already painted piece and then drop in Fluid Acrylics (any colors) and drag the toothpick through for additional interest and a highly shiny surface.

Clear Tar Gel   Self Leveling
                   Clear Gel

Weave Acrylic Skins

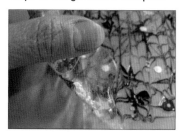

1. Spread gel in a rectangular or square area onto HDPE plastic or freezer paper. Add color by dropping in Fluid Acrylics. Move the drops in wet gel with a toothpick.

2. Allow to dry thoroughly until all non-painted areas of the gel are <u>clear</u>, not white or cloudy.

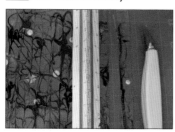

3. Peel off the "skin". Lay it on a cutting surface, then use a ruler and mat or craft knife to cut the skin into long strips.

4. Weave the strips together, over and under fashion. Apply as a collage element using Soft Gel (Gloss) as the "glue".

Make variations in colors.

Variation: Tint Clear Tar Gel with Fluid Acrylics and use this colored gel to drip onto an HDPE surface spread with untinted gel. Allow to dry. Peel off the skin to mount on top of a painting, or mount it temporarily on a window and watch the light shine through the colors.

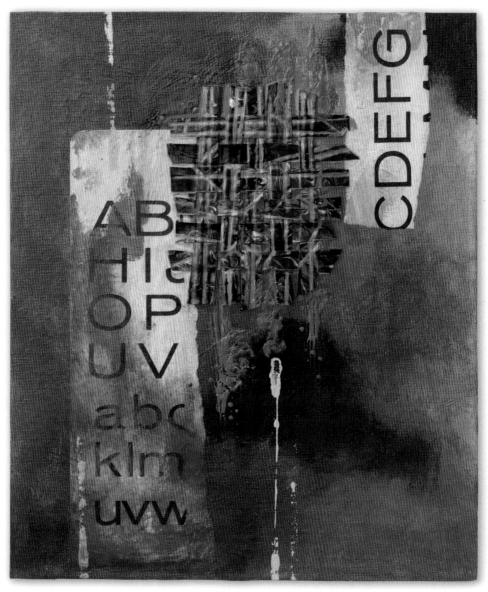

Woven Strips of Clear Tar Gel "Skin": Make a "Black" ground, then collage elements. Apply stains and glazes to create a beautiful background. Weave a section of Clear Tar Gel "skins". Apply the weaving with Soft Gel (Gloss). Add additional brushstrokes of Green Gold for detail.

Create stunning and shimmering effects on handmade cards.

Shimmering Iridescents

The metallic look has a richness that is all its own. Metal looks precious and expensive so gold, copper, silver and bronze make perfect highlights.

Truly Mixed Media... I created this beautiful abstract piece from all "leftover" items. I used a paper towel (printed with little circular dots) to clean up spilled Airbrush Quinacridone Magenta, allowed it to dry, then used Soft Gel (Gloss) to glue the towel to a board for the background. I also applied a scrap of origami mesh with Soft Gel (Gloss).

The other elements are "skins" of leftover paints and glazes that I used for other artwork in this book. Next I overpainted the areas with Fluid Acrylics and Airbrush Acrylics.

For the final touch I added the "skins" of Clear Tar Gel mixed with Iridescent Gold.

Use Acrylic Ground for Pastels as a texture medium on a board and allow to dry. Stain the surface with a Dioxazine Purple glaze and allow to dry. Finally push Iridescent Gold through a stencil and add collage elements.

Shimmering Iridescents

Iridescents create marvelous metallic colors and surfaces... and the best part, they won't tarnish like many real metals.

Stamped dots and leaves glimmer and form great color.

Stamped alphabet creates glistening shapes on these special cards.

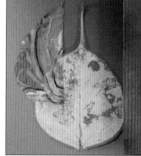

Paint Fluid Acrylics on Gessoed canvas, allow to dry, then drip swirls of Iridescent Bright Gold right from the bottle.

Apply a "Skin" Over Iridescents for a Great Look!

For a special effect, add a bit of swirl in a "skin" with Self Leveling Clear Gel and Fluid Acrylics over an Iridescent Bronze leaf.

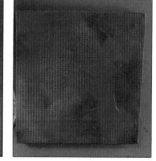

1. Start with a painted canvas, a preserved leaf painted Iridescent Bronze, and a skin with Self Leveling Clear Gel and Interference Fluids. • 2. Adhere the leaf to the canvas with Soft Gel (Gloss). Allow to dry.

3. Adhere the "skin" to the leaf on the canvas using Soft Gel again. • 4. Outline the leaf with Black Fluid Acrylic using a fine brush.

"Embossed Tiles"
Light Molding Paste and Clear Tar Gel with Fluid Acrylics

Light Molding Paste makes a great textured white. Add color to it for a textured tint/pastel.

Apply Light Molding Paste. Allow to dry. Then wet the surface of the paste with water and add Fluid Color. You will see the color spread out over the surface and bloom in front of your eyes. If you allow the surface to dry in between color applications, you can repeat this process for additional depth of color.

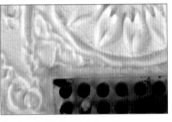

1. Apply Light Molding Paste.

2. Wet the surface with water.

3. Drop in transparent colors.

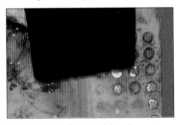

4. Rewet surface, add Iridescent colors.

5. Coat with Clear Tar Gel.

Rich and Glossy Embossed "Tiles"

1. Apply Light Molding Paste evenly to a 6" square canvas board. Push a foam stamp pattern (*Making Memories* stamp) into the paste while wet and lift out immediately. Don't worry if the pattern is not "perfect" at this point. This takes practice and you should try it a few times. Remember to clean any excess paste off the stamp with warm soapy water and an old toothbrush. Allow to dry thoroughly. • 2. Wet the surface of the dry Light Molding Paste "tile" with plain water. Be generous but do not soak. You can always add extra water as needed. • 3. Begin to drop in modern transparent colors (stick to a tight color family, Quinacridone Red, Magenta and Violet for example) for a ceramic glaze-like effect. The colors will spread out through the paste. Pick 3 compatible colors to start with, and cover the tile leaving some small areas of white showing. Let dry thoroughly. • 4. Rewet surface and add in Iridescent Colors (Gold, Bright Gold) of your choice compatible with your prior color choices. Make sure to cover all of the white areas with this paint. Allow to dry thoroughly. • 5. Coat the entire "tile" with a generous amount of Clear Tar Gel using a palette knife to pull it across the surface of the "Tile". Allow to dry thoroughly.

More Tips and Tricks

"Poppies Under Plastic"

Bury layers of texture under Clear Tar Gel. Enhance the finished piece with a final "scrape" of bright color!

This glowing collage piece has lots of texture and drama. Adhere a Rose transfer into Glass Bead Gel. Scrape Iridescent Silver over the areas of Glass Bead Gel to add highlights.

Make Something out of Nothing:

Save your scraps from old books and newspapers. Embellish your piece with left-over decorative papers. You can paint and glaze right over the images and words.

See what you can do.

Use a palette knife to scrape color over a slick painted surface. This will add texture and interest on a canvas or board.

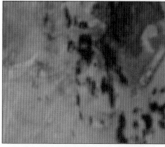

When using a stencil, always apply product or paint in one direction to keep the liquid or polymer gel from seeping under the stencil.

Remove immediately and allow to dry.

Photos always add charm and memories to cards. Black and white copies of photos and transparencies add a great personal touch.

Capture Your Family History

Capture your memories by incorporating photos into your artwork. From cards and canvas, to Altered Books, sketchbooks and scrapbook pages, everything looks great with the addition of color.

My studio is brimming with collage pieces that tell stories about the people and experiences I have encountered, many enriched with pieces of family history. I am often commissioned by families and I begin each piece with an interview to capture the story to be told on the canvas.

Glaze and Color Pages in Altered Books:

Colorful glazes and paints work really well in Altered Books and on ATCs. Create textures with resist and pastes, paint colors as a checkerboard or door in the background, or add tints to black and white photocopies. Whatever you want to do, Polymer Mediums and Fluid Colors will do the job.

The best choice for photos in collage is lazer or toner-based copies of black and white photos because they will not alter or fade like color photos. Add glazes over the surface for color.

Create Personalized Scrapbook Paper:

A great idea and fun to do, too! Decorate your own scrapbook paper in any color or design.

Push Molding Paste through a stencil onto 140 lb. cold press watercolor paper. Paint and glaze the background with Heavy Body Acrylics and/or Fluid Acrylics. Use foam stamps to add additional designs. Allow to dry, then add photos and scrapbook embellishments.

Scrapbook page by Paula Phillips.